READ O

See

by Lada Josefa Kratky

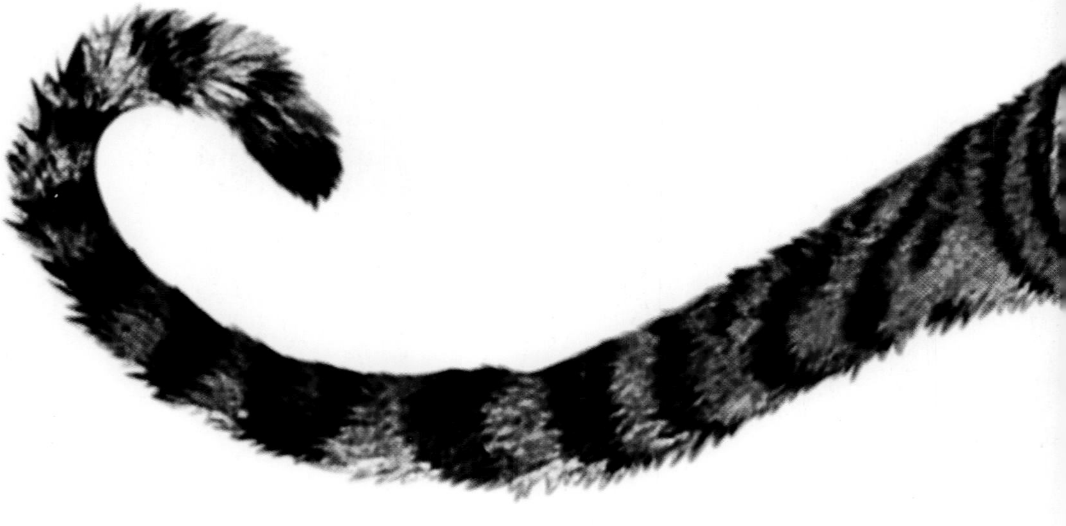

NATIONAL GEOGRAPHIC

School Publishing

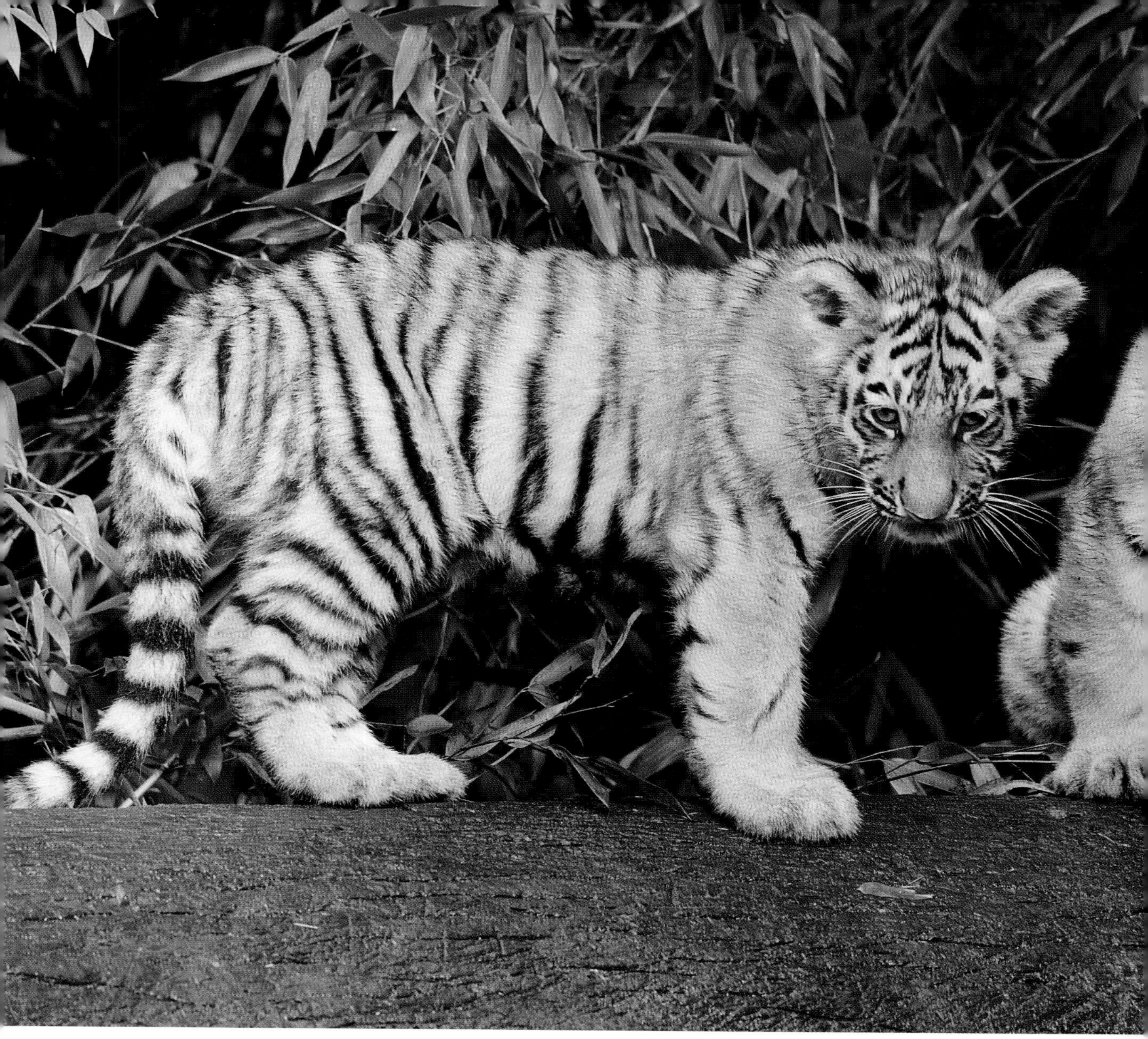

See a 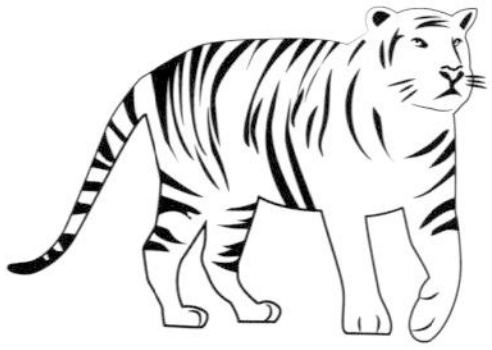 .

tiger

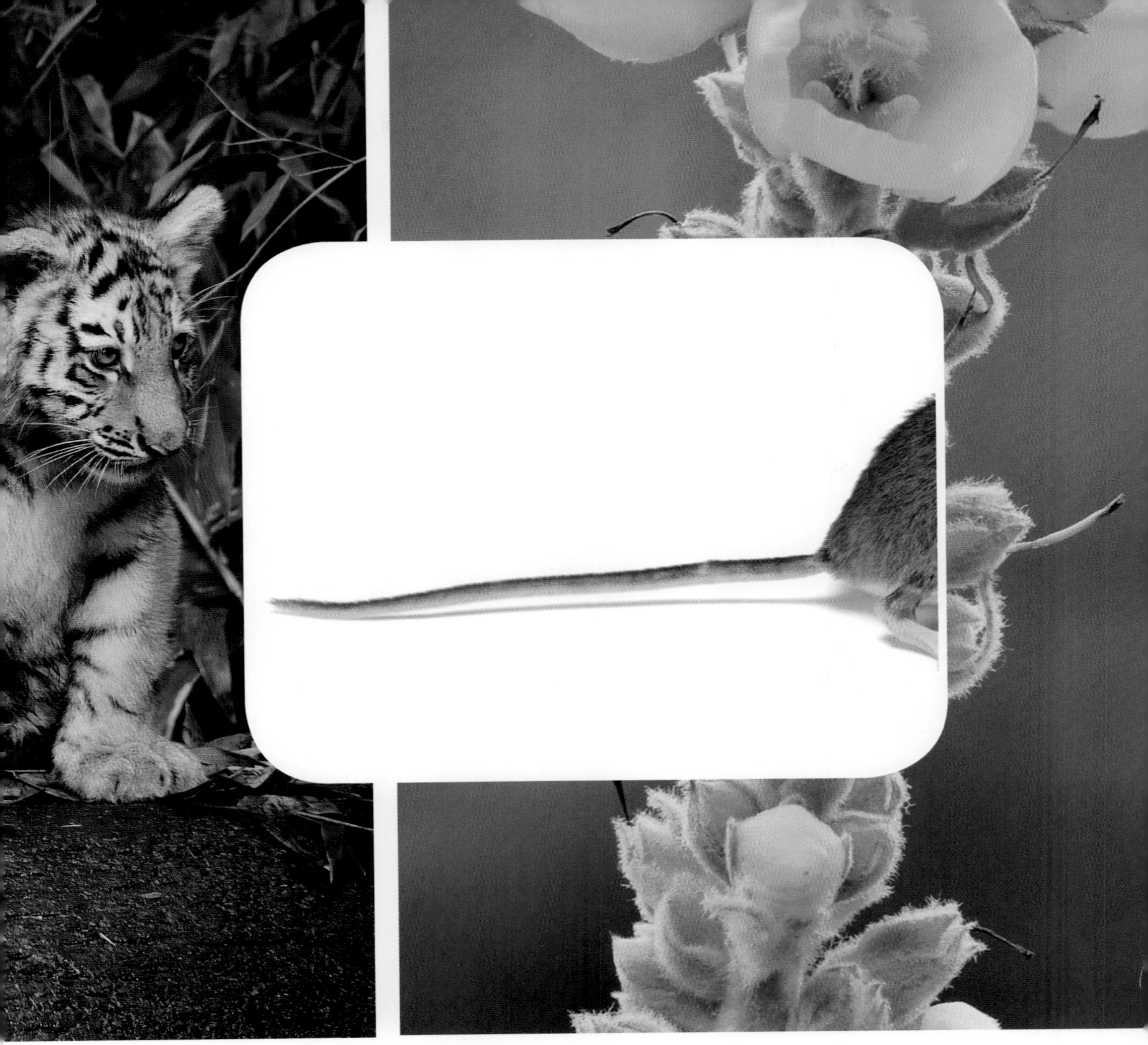

See a 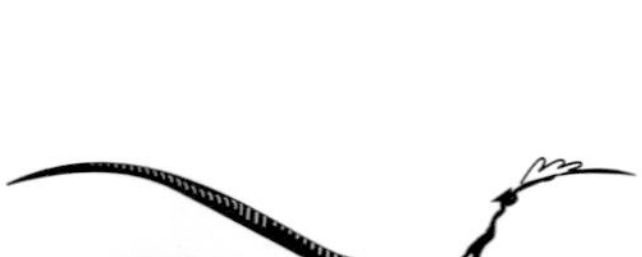 .

tail

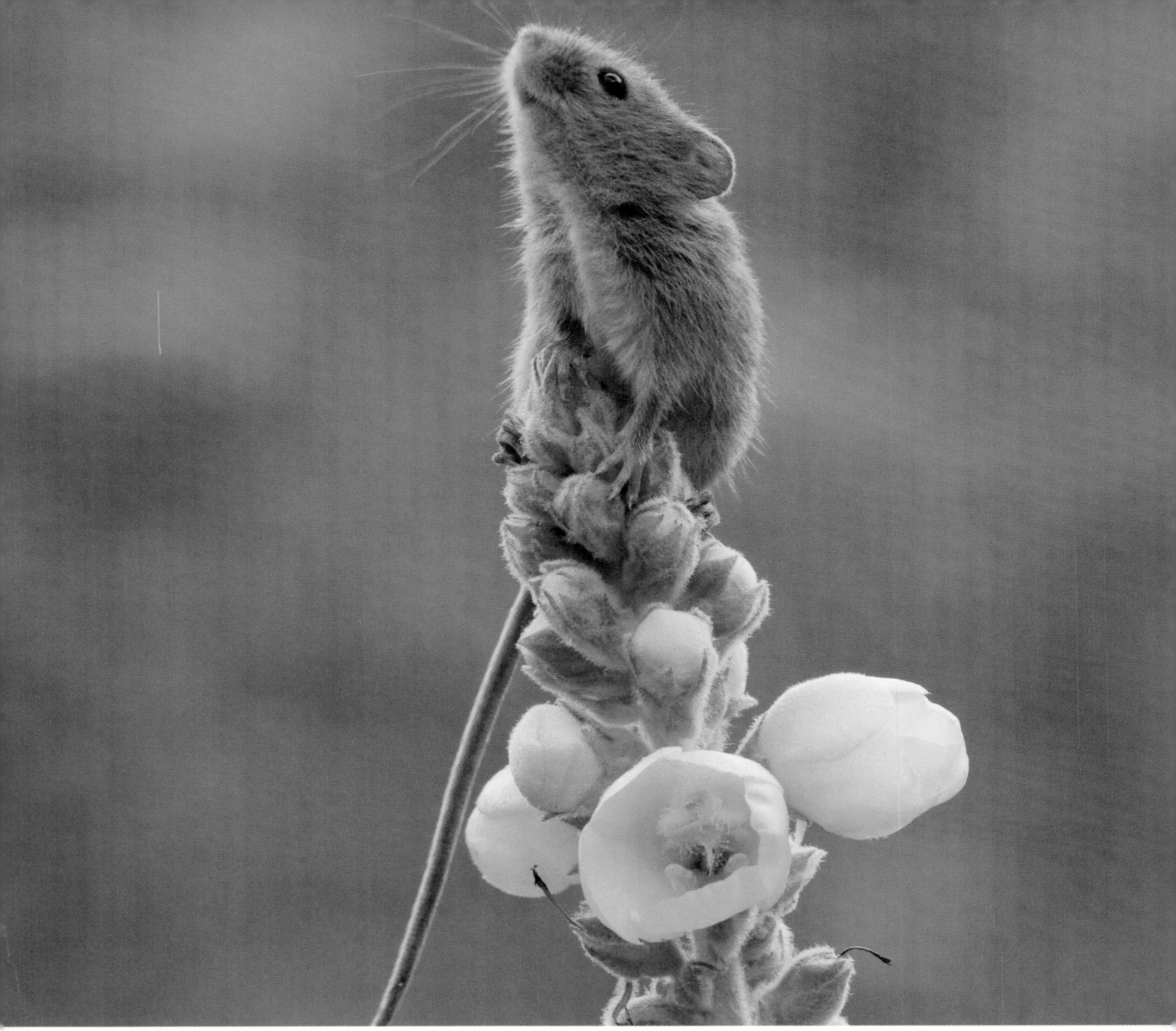

See a 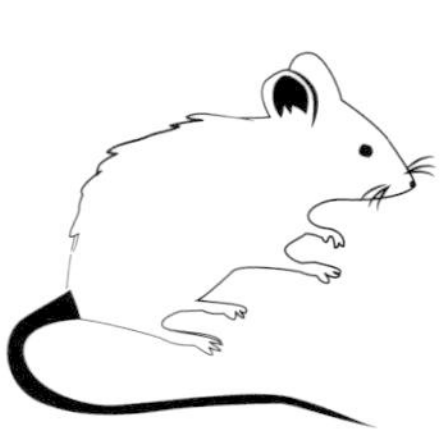 .

rat

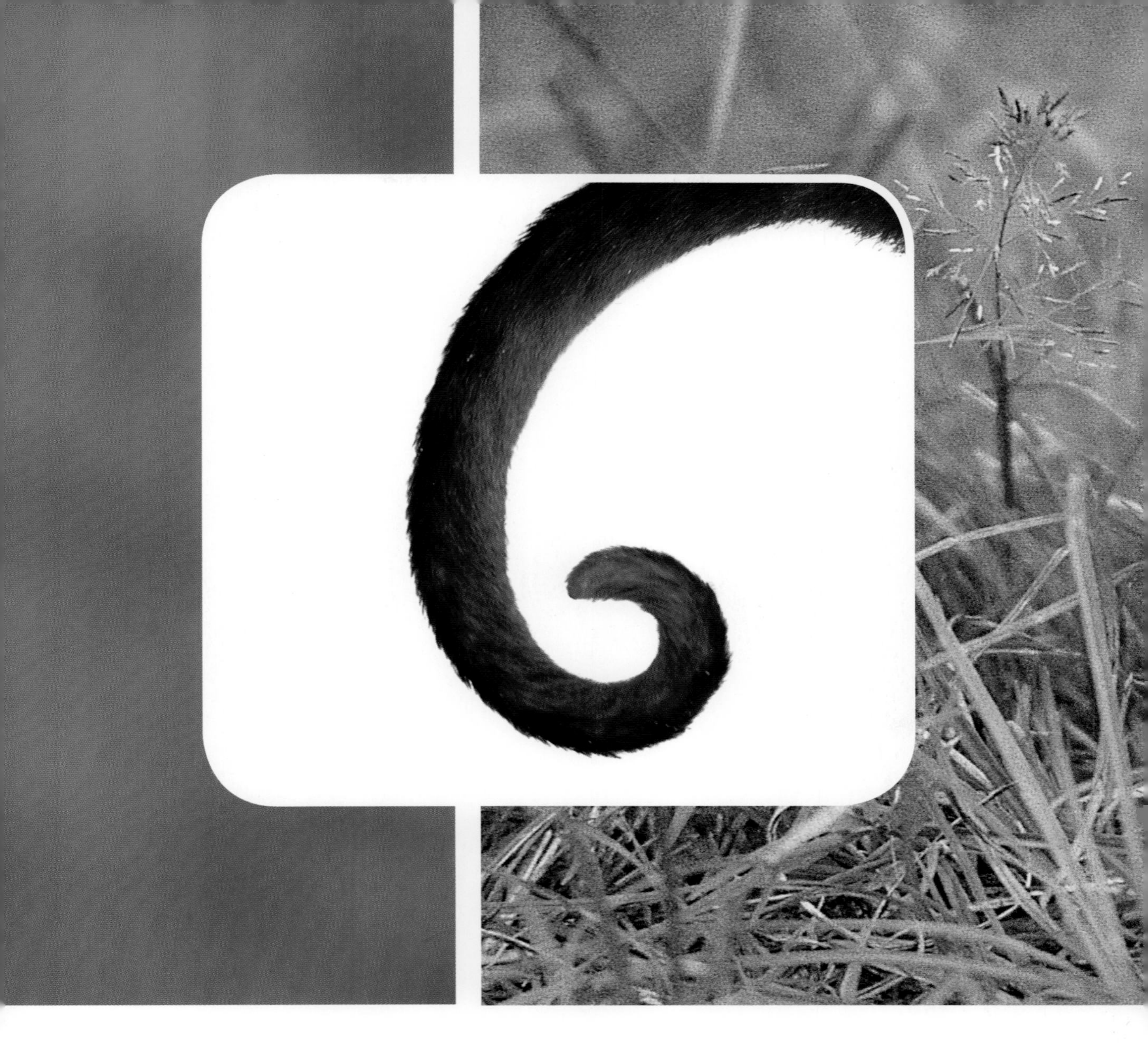

See a 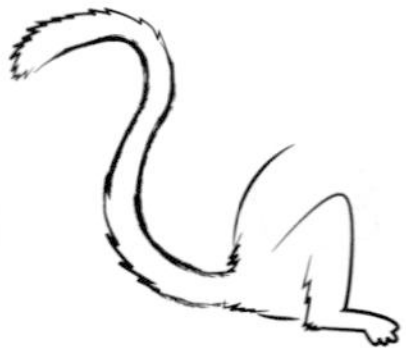 .

tail

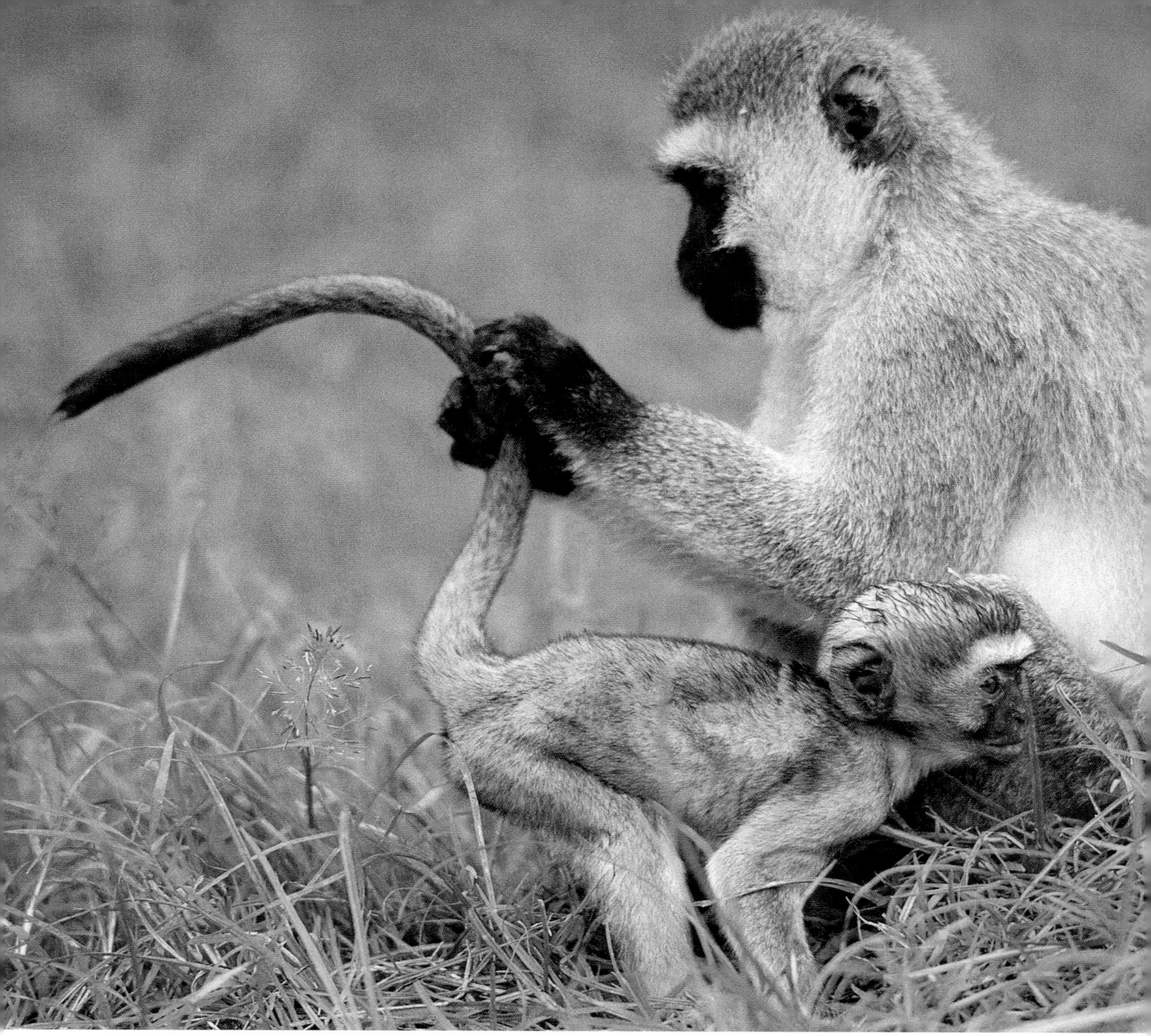

See a 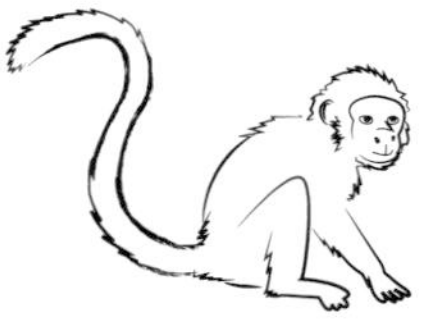 .

monkey

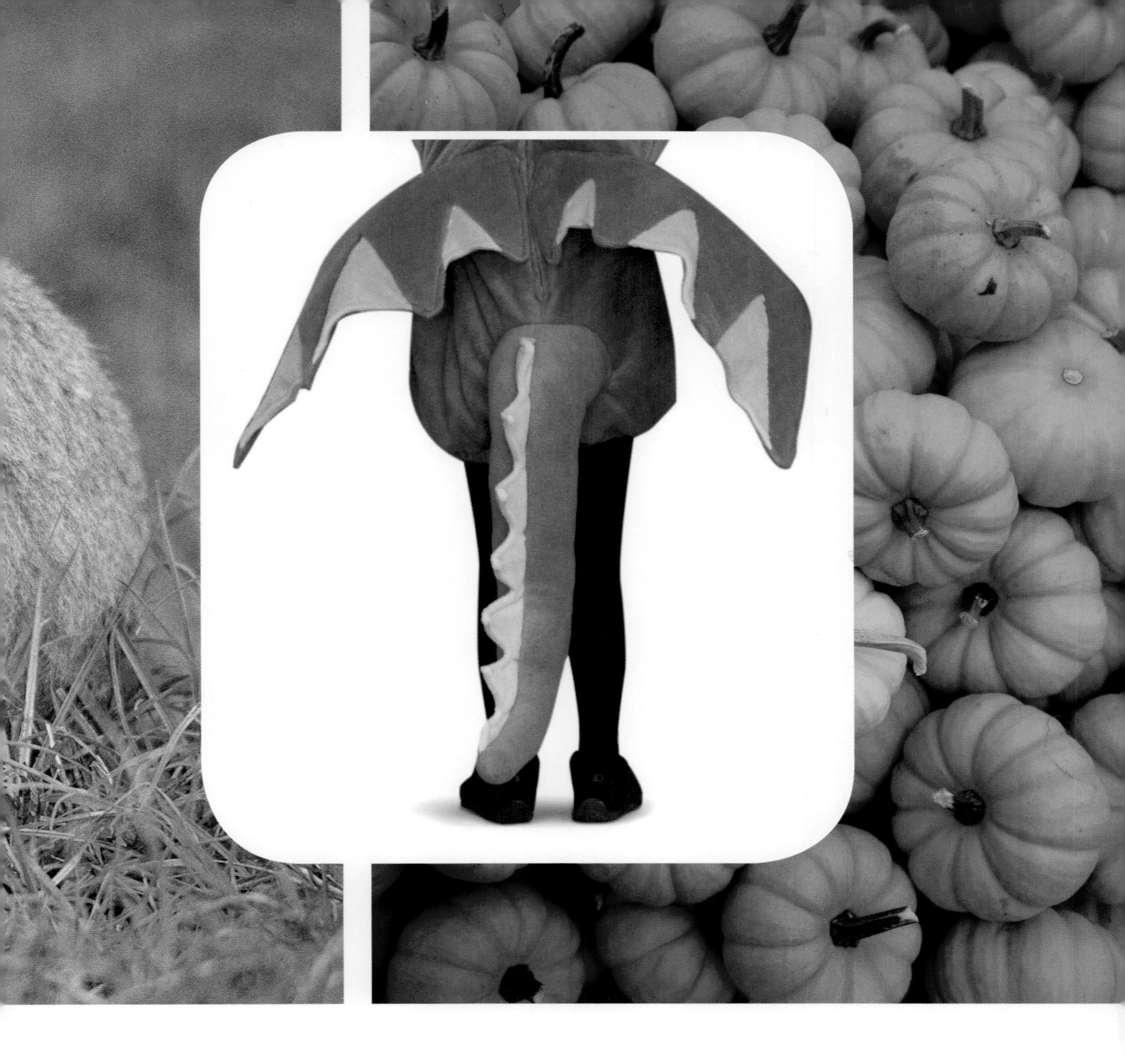

See a 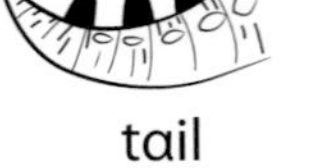 .

tail

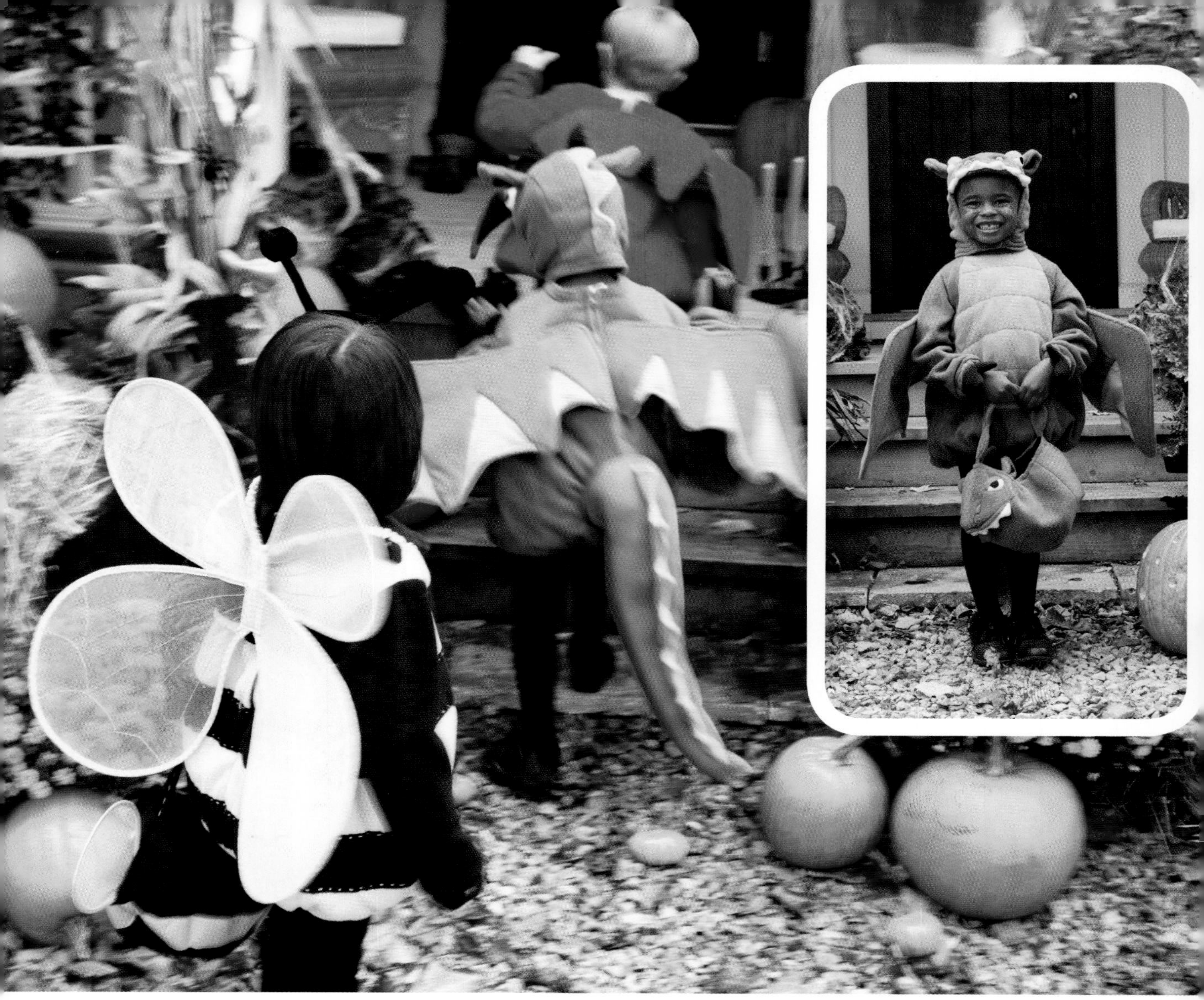

See a 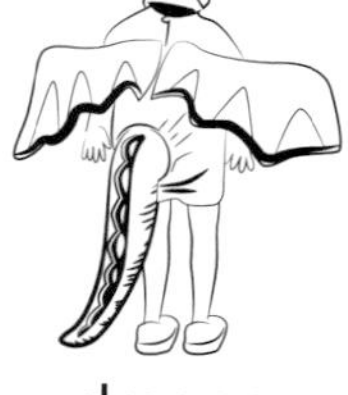 .

dragon

See a 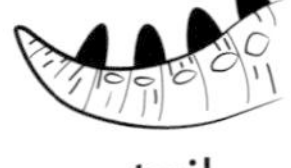 .

tail